# A Gangster's GUIDE To KEEPING HER

## A Series of Services
### By Terrance Hutson

LinesToLife.Com

A Gangster's GUIDE To KEEEPING HER Copyright© 2021 LinesToLife.Com, LLC All rights reserved

No part of this publication may be reproduced, distributed or transmitted in any form or by any means, including photocopying, recording or other electronic or mechanical methods, without the prior written permission of the publisher, except in the case of brief quotation embodied in reviews and certain other non-commercial uses permitted by copyright law.

ISBN:978-1-7367937-2-5

## Table of Contents

The Preface - 1

A Few Things To Understand First - 3

The First Ouchies - 12

Learning How To Love - 22

WTF You Tryna Say - 31

Know You, You Know - 39

You Chose Her - 44

I Tried Hella Times - 48

You Are The Center Of It All - 53

That Sh!t Could've Been Avoided - 58

The Gift - 63-69

Everything Is Okay, Now - 70

# A Gangster's Guide to Keeping Her
By Terrance Hutson
## THE PREFACE

Okay. I, myself, am not sure if anyone can be 'kept'. I do believe, deep down, we've, all, wished it possible. From the first taste of liking. To the, initial, moment when you fake surprisingly said, 'I love you.' To the instant you wanted to be sexy for and to her. We all, thought, 'hell yeah, this the one', head ass. For alwaaays and foreveerrr,' face ass. But reality stepped in and smacks you all the way back to the present. Now you and Cameo, asking, why have I lost you? At times, Loving her can make you say, heaven must be like this. Word to OP. Then there are those times. The moments when yo, lousy ass, can't make sense of, why she still fucking with you? For the one's that have cleaned up the debris of emotional rubble. For those of you, who have always, lived tidy. Also, for the men and young men, that have, just recently, found themselves in something new and good. This Guide is for you.

Again, this is not a guide, boasting I can knock any woman and know how to keep her. And you're a damned fool, to think that I think that I, do know. But what it is, is me carrying a hand full of experiences to help me present a gift of a little bit of wisdom. Plus, some references to R&B songs and love ballads on Keeping her important. Keeping her liked on. Keeping her fucked on. Keeping her informed. Keeping her in mind. Keeping her benefiting. Keeping her, interested, in you. Keeping her happy, with you. Keeping her communicating, for all involved. Keeping her knowing you care for her. Do you see a trend, yet? Keeping her from embarrassment. Keeping her out of drama. Keeping her cool. If she's cool. And you're cool? Then shit's cool.

# A Gangster's Guide To Keeping Her
By Terrance Hutson
## A Few Things To Understand, 1ˢᵗ

First. I am not telling you that I am an expert or a pro, regarding the affairs of the heart. I am not. Plus, I ain't kept a goddamn thang. And single, right now. However, I do know, love or loving is the best part of us. And the best in us. It is the root to our power source of being Godlike or of God's image. Respecting that fact should help us perform better, in and with Love. Two. I will not claim to have all the answers, for you. But you can trust that I have been in and screwed up enough relationships to know what should not happen. And what needs to take place, for a now and a future. In this guide, I am speaking to you from a, 'How to enjoy living in love, with your person,' type of position. I know I know what love is. I, truly, believe I've been in love, before. Maybe two or thirteen times. You know. But who's keeping count? Yet and still, yes. I do know good love. Even though, they'd never noticed my love. The real love I, actually, possess for my her. It was as if, they would be courting themselves. The ones I've claimed, were only interested in how I could or would treat them. Without thinking twice about the love needs of mine. It always felt like, whoever, 'she' was and I were both dating, 'her'. Me, being a "gangster," probably, made it difficult for someone to see the, almost, most perfect man, was for and in front of them. Then, me having this 'tough guy' energy, most of their challenges was figuring out if my hard core would rule and ruin the relationship by trying to control it.

The 'My way or the highway' mentality was never my take. Especially, when it came to the success of a healthy pairing. I wasn't versed in the compromising side of togetherness. But I was aware of it. And sure, I should do more than just notice the flaw. I thought I did, do more. I, really, wanted to make her happy. All of them, for that matter. I just needed something back from and out of My love, too. At the time, I didn't acknowledge this fact. But as a man, I believed the things I've said and shown, was me being accommodating to her points. Then, one day I had an epiphany. When could I ever perform an emotional trade-off, if I associated bargaining as the first sign of conceding? Unless, I started to look at the same thing differently. I could never offer her a give and take setting. How do I turn down me enough to surrender such vulnerabilities? Do I have to make myself less or unimportant to have 'my her'? It took me a while to find the most sensible answers. But I found them. I'll share those later. In all of my relationships, it seemed like I was to be at her disposal. Not a helpmate. So, I harped on how not to be. How ,not, to make myself look, sound, act or walk like a fucking sucka. I won't be a, for shit. And where I'm from, sucka shit is yielding. Yielding is relinquishing. To relinquish is to fold. And niggas ain't folding. Aw naw. None of that. Where I'm from. Now, how does a person, with that thinking, expect to keep a, 'her'? I shouldn't expect shit. Yet, I still tried. Hella times.

    Expectations. Hmm. Ain't this some shit? I wanted to live, this life, with no expectations of any other person. I wasn't this way, trying to avoid disappointment. Not necessarily. I took this approach, to eliminate adding pressure to an already delicate thing. The frangibility of loving can not endure, that, which is not of love. According to the receiver. But since we, all, can be considered receivers, who, then, is left to give? This type of shit is what makes loving fragile. The fine line, balancing act of giving and receiving. I've, probably, taken damned near, every relationship situation for granted. In some manner, I'm sure of it. Intentionally? Fuck no. But the foul doesn't care for your intent. When the foul was committed. And from that an individual can have you up on that charge. Without calling upon the witness of purity in your heart. Now, the loss hurts, so much more. Because the evidence of intent is inadmissible. Meaning, the only thing, literally and figuratively, noticed is the foul. No prior testimony nor any consideration for your, fairly, clean record will be reviewed in your case. Expectations are not, fully, understood. I see the setup and self afflictions suffered from it. I also see the reasoning and benefit behind setting or having them. Expecting more from yourself, brings the logic of expecting more of/for yourself and others. If you don't want shit? You won't get shit or be shit. But what will never work is that one-sided shit. The taking of but not returning the goodness. Or being the good giver and you getting the short stick.

But with you being and seeing yourself in something good. That, alone, creates the willingness to have the ability to compromise. And/or vice versa. The ability to be willing does sprout from such an environment, too. The moral of this part of the story is simple. Take care of one another. Don't put too much emphasis on what you don't know, haven't experienced or how you ain't. No. Chill. And see if you can see yourself as the most relaxed you've ever been around your person? You can't fake this one. Once your spirit is settled, try to feel the energies that are there and be guided. For some, you may be closer to that place. Others, you may have to help you stay conscious of getting there. But you can. It took me hella long. But my walk is not yours. I came from broken. I never knew better. I only knew me. And The Town. The things that I am able to tell you, today, mothafuckas didn't tell us, growing up. It was, "hey, go out and do all the most dangerously dumb ass shit y'all can do." "After that go place weenie in the middle of every woman on earth." "Then, go to the California Youth Authority, go to jail and you better go to prison after that." "And now you a G." Not a Man. But whatever the fuck a 'G' is. I'm that, to another nigga. And to a dummy, like me, this was good shit. And prestigious.

 This 'gangster' shit stemmed from tons of set ups in my surroundings. The drama and trauma turned me into an aggressive, confrontational, thinking and watching, protective mechanism. Alpha shit. Then people's misinformation about Alphas (male/female), has trained me to expect to remain misunderstood, judged and alone. In my attempts to provide clarity and assistance, I want you to let my honesty about my life, help you. With that being said. Again. I wasn't able or equipped to keep nobody. Some shit, I'm to blame. Other shit, I saw fault. I held the blame because I didn't think I needed to change. And I still don't. My core is beautiful. I am a way like none other. Facts! But can I learn things I could apply to this life? Definitely. But can, you or they and them, learn from me? For sure. But my way of teaching is, "too aggressive,"or "your delivery comes off like.." And now I can't be. Or communicate because the focus has shifted. And then, you'll be saying, I've changed. Like you don't know why and shit. Being a better human is something I think everybody aspires to be. I know me. I love that man of me. Will our internal battles ever cease? While we are alive? I don't know. But if those battles, with ourselves end, will that make us stop trying to be better? To me, that would go against my natural understanding.

    Understanding who you are, will help you determine your likes and dislikes. What you will do. Versus what you won't. In turn, knowing you, will lead and guide you into your comfort levels, with others and life. Which, helps you build your compatibility charts. Filtering who and what's allowed in your realms of peace. For goodness' sake. Say that you are a kindhearted person. Most likely, you're going to want to seek out someone with kind qualities. If your hustling and grinding skills are way up. Should your partner's? Or shouldn't that match? You see what I'm getting at? I used to think we needed to be with our opposite. The yin to a yang thingy. Now, I believe the yin/yang is, actually, woman and man. And that's the opposite. Not the idea of, if I'm a sweetheart, I need a thug ass chick. Maybe, she is highly intelligent. Does this mean she needs an idiot? To balance it out? Nah. What makes more sense, to me, now, is that a couple should simply be synced up. Meaning, being aligned with you guys' jobs in the relationship. The shit I was on, as far as a mate, was some silly ass surface level ignorance. She had to be physically attractive and meek. I can't say her physical wealth, is not important, at all. But I can say it does not rank high, with me, anymore. I've been told, I'm fine as the fuck. To this day. But for me, now, she just has to be willing. I am.

    As an Alpha, your job is to hold it down. In all aspects. That's a gang of pressure. Even if you can handle the whole load. Stress, depression and other excuses made me fumble the ball.

Then at one point, my finances took a dive. And a lady I loved love, used my rough time against me. Not in the sense of reverse psychology. To trick a nigga into getting his shit back together. Nope. She added a skanless ass degradation to the game. Piercing through shit. I let that pin me down, as I waddled in my shitty pity. On top of the other punk shit, I was going through. For me, being together, has to mean, we lift and encourage one another. If your person is tearing you down, with mental and verbal abuse? That is Not your person. My process for the bounce back is shared, plainly, in 'A Gangster's Guide To Goodness.' However, I will say this. Having a connection to something bigger, whether it's only on your inside or it's wide open. Knowing your part of the 'big', you're involved with, lends an amazing power. And once you've tapped into it, nothing can relieve you of it.

The peeks and glances of caring, I did witness. Made me know I was being loved on. I've had hella chances to look into the eyes of loving. Attempting to mimic its gaze. Trying to reflect its reciprocation. I've heard the voice of convincing adulation. Clearly, articulate the intentions of desire. I've seen the sexiest actions put into attraction, with no effort. I've stood smack dab in the middle of the beauty of love's pull. The remarkable impression, this feeling has locked around my life, authorizes me, to assertively, tell my truths. One definite truth, is that I am a romantically traumatized fuck. I am fucked up in the head, right now, from wanting things one way and seeing them make a left, for no, apparent, fucking reason. The emotional anguish, caused by a breakup can have lingering and damaging effects on your outlook. These, few, memories are not baggage. These initial stories are to help you see how my pains and triumphs, qualify me as the speaker. From a gangster's guide to keeping her.

# A Gangster's Guide To Keeping Her
By Terrance Hutson
## The First Ouchies

The year was 1987. The scene, North Oakland. Carter Middle School. And there, in front of my class, the new girl stood. As the teacher introduced the new girl, I was already hers. My goodness. Just her being, informed me, in that moment, I had a type. Her. Fourteen year old me(Yes. Fucking 14. My b-day was after the school session began). Any damn way. 14 year old me, saw her as the most beautiful thing in all of the Americas. To me, she was. Long, thick, dark hair. Big ass brown eyes. A smile, wrapped in the full lips of a goddess. That smile, held the power to capture a soul, forever. Once my scary ass moved passed being moved by this anomaly. I was honest, with her, about liking her. And she liked me back. We hung out, a lot. Dances. The Lake. Eastmont. At each other's houses. We were little ass kids, really in like, like a mug.

Then one day, out of the blue, she dumped me. At halftime. At one of my games. I was just in. I asked, why? As I'm choking the shit out of my tear ducts. I was hurting. But not a drop better fall from a mothafuckin' eyeball. Not in front of her. Then she gave the why. I was left for this silly ass, fake tough guy. Because he sold dope and had the bad guy image. Those were her words, exactly. Girls were into the bad boys, then. Shit. It's probably still a thing, now. At the time, I, myself, was a part of a young team from West Oakland. Getting dope money, hitting little licks, fighting clowns and "bustin' at them bustas, on a mothafuckin' 10 speed". Shout out Bad Influenz. But I would, damned near, be a model student in class. A hella hard ass nerd, for real. No one knew about the dirt. Nobody was supposed to know. Plus, I didn't need everybody knowing. I came this close to saying, ' hold up, hold up, lil ol' beezy, I do that shit too.' But I could not. My new girl wanted a new guy. I gave her my back. And a lonely, traitorous ass tear tracked down my face. I was big hurt. But the respect she earned from me, that day, remains, today. She did something as a kid, grown folks wasn't even doing. Being straight up and honest. And more than 30 years later, we are still, hella cool hella cool. Yes. The knife of pain left me with a wound. But an education, as well. From that, one of the coldest niggas on earth was birthed.

    Not the 'coldest' like there was a grudge attached. Nah. Though, it was the first thought I had, to remedy or reverse my emotional damage.

But that's not me, fam. What I mean when I say, the 'coldest', is the way the next relationship will be approached. I knew then, what I know now. While most people are shallow thinkers and it reflects in their speech. And their actions. I've always been more appropriate for the layers and levels of this life. The more I'd cater to this ability, the more understanding I was granted. With the understanding came a trust, the ladies could have in my words. And from that, I was gifted a rare believability. Ladies loved. So, when I gave them my thug and a gentleman shit, the difference was welcomed. A couple of years passed. In between those years, I flirted with a lot of girls and got numbers. But when it came to claiming a girlfriend, I refused.

Then my homegirl, Tonya, from O High, introduced me to her friend. A slim, high yellow girl. She was modelesque. With the juiciest lips on the planet, gotdamnit. After Tonya threatened me within the, "Don't hurt my friend," spiel. I wanted to prove, to Tonya, I would never hurt her best friend. Who is, now, my new friend. And at first, I was going to make sure I kept my word to Tonya. Rest in Peace, baby. But my homegirl's homegirl, was so beyond this galaxy. It was easy to fall for her. And to be in love with her. She had a good mix of niceness and spunk. Her sense of humor, aw man. And she was still a virgin. I kept trying to let her make it, man. I was trying to save her, from me. The me who, months prior, had a group of females, openly and knowingly, hold competitions to see which one was I going to hit, first. Yes. First. This was a real thing. Hey. I used to belong to them streeeeheheeheeets. For real.

Peep, though. Have you ever known or met a person, you wanted to make them feel safe, always? Or you just wanted to keep them away from the madness? And they wasn't yo family member? She was that person, for me. I would come up to her school. Ride the bus with her to her house. And I had a car. Her dad wasn't going for that. His baby, in a closed space, like a car? With some little nigga. That's a hell's naw. I would, sometimes, get her and her younger brother dinner. Mostly Cybelles pizza. It was, sometimes, because her dad didn't want her accepting things from boys. And he and I were cool as a fan. One time, I slapped the dog shit out of 2 dummies, talking reckless. So, her father didn't risk going to jail, for doing it himself. I was loyal and faithful, to her, as a youngin. Mainly, so karma wouldn't take me out for not recognizing and respecting one of earth's angel. I never pressed her for her virginity, either. Ever. It wasn't til later in life, when she blessed me with some of the sweetest love, I've ever known. We gave each other another piece of us to remember. But I'm telling you, I really tried to save her from me and dudes like me. She loved me, for real, for that. Then, I let us down. Behind some stupid ass street shit.

    I never got fronted dope. My young team, we bought ours. One day, the plug flipped on me. He wanted to front us. Which meant more money all around. But at an extra cost, though. And I, for one, wasn't fucking with no extra nothing. The plug got to acting like a bitch. Because I said no to the offer. He began to threaten harm and my life. I didn't trip. Then, that motherfucker called the house. Telling my Mom what they were going to do to her oldest son. She wanted to send me away. To keep me alive. This meant, I had to leave my virgin, too. Now, I'm tripping. And he put my Mom in it. None of you niggas scare or have ever pumped a fragment of fear in my fucking heart. Because I will kill you niggas. Straight up. They kept playing. I kept it real real. I blessed the threat. And dipped for a bit, without the virgin's knowledge. I popped back up a year or so later. To find out she didn't live in the same spot. I had to stop searching. Hella years later, I saw her on Fruitvale and MacArthur. She was still the same beautiful. Except, now, she is thick as the fuck fuck. SHIT! And the way she held me, I felt how much she loved me, still. For that I will, always, love her, back.

I've had my share of girl and lady friends. The one thing I've had the ability to do, is be a true friend. But I would give more of a friend level care to my her. And not the level of caring from the romantic side of the game. I had no idea I was missing it. I never liked made-up, make believe shit. Or playing with folks. Especially, folks' feels. To me, you and I, ain't 'we' til marriage. So, 'going together,' ain't shit, for real. This being my mindset, I've loved from a pure place. One of friendship. And I brought all of the characteristics of a good friend. Mix that in with the intimacies of a passionate and aggressive lover. I had this dating shit, in the bag. To some, my ways and beliefs sound like the perfect mate. But there is no perfect. There is only the best, One, for you. And you responding as the best, one, for that person. Again, knowing yourself, makes most of this shit look easy. Being honest about my shit, owning it, helped keep me in a real placement in the hearts of lovers gone. Just not in their lives.

Well, not in the physical sense. But the experiences of a me will, forever, be remembered. Most of them doubled back. Mostly to confess, wishing they had listened to me. Or wished they could've seen, the real, at the time.

Let me be clear with you. Please, don't call it cap, either. I've forgotten or turned down more women than most men have ever even talked to. Yet, so private, I was never given the reputation as a 'ladies man.' You would hear how hell of them liked me. But nothing off putting about my rep, though. I learned my lesson of what hurting someone, looked like, a while ago. So, that example curved any desire to introduce intentional bullshit into another person's life. The combinations of hurt and embarrassment. Disappointment and sadness. On one face? Broke my heart, too. And I don't wish for anybody to know the feeling of that pain. Nor the helplessness you feel, knowing you can't ease that pain. You caused. I will protect us, by using the most common sense rule, ever. "DO Unto Others.." And giving, exactly, what I expect. While refusing to accept some shit that I am not giving you. The energies you put out, will be returned to you. My respect and belief in good and bad karma, mean enough, to me, to stay solid. No matter the circumstances.

Before I get deeper in how to keep her, listen. A couple more years roll by. I'm maturing, some what. I'm back home from the road. Between a little music stuff and some weed stuffed, I was across the nation. Now that I'm in Oakland. I have to hit up, one, of my favorite spots. The Serenader. My folks went the weekend prior but I was gone. I get to the bar. The first people I see, are mines. One of my, real, folks introduced me to a lady that he knew. After I paid for her and our drinks, my mans disappeared. Her and I just stood there. I ran my eyes across her landscape, like search lights. Looking for a spot I could hide. She was too sexy for t.v. Tall, 5'11" and thick as the fuck. My size. Her skin was a completely and evenly coated milk chocolate toned. Nigga! I Love milk chocolate. It's my favorite. Say, you know how women can do some subtle little shit? How she's seated. She nibbles, a bit, on the tip of a straw. The interest in her laughter. It could be anything. But it's the most attractive or sexiest shit you've ever seen? This is what I got, with her. She used to do this thing with her eyes squinted. Face angled, in a slight tilt. As her half smile let her teeth tips hold her bottom lip in a habitual position of seduction. Oh my gosh, nigga. This Amazon? Stallion? Whatever you should call her. She did it for me. This was a grown ass lady. I think I may have been 23 -24. She was 36. And was the total package. She worked hard and had fun. She ran her own business and made paper. She was my kind of fine. And a Libra, like me. On top of an immediate, mutual attraction, I believed, the Libra thing ultra connected us. Time went on. Her and I became an item. We did seem to fit. From our personalities to our sexual freedoms. She matched my vibe. She matched my D. She matched.

Then one day, for some hating ass reason, her fat ass niece lied on me. Out of her presumptions and assumptions. I did have a female at my house. That wasn't the lie. The lie told, was me and my homegirl of decades was fucking. We, absolutely, were not. Everybody, including my Match, knew that I wrote or helped write on projects, around the bay. And Oakland, for sure. The big beezy lived in the same building as I did. I had no clue she lived over here. I didn't do nothing so I didn't give a shit where she stayed. I couldn't tell you a thing about her. Because I'm not watching anybody. But they watching me, though. My

Match, took this lie as fact. It messed me up up. I wanted to ask, how could and why would you believe this, about me? Me, of All people? But I needed to, not ask. I had no use for an answer. Just more trust. What's hella sad? She wrote me a letter and taped it to my car windshield. She explained why she acted as if she didn't believe me. I opened it and it read,

*"I am so sorry. I know you didn't do anything, with that chick. I wanted your conscience to be freed of that. I have to tell you something, I never wanted you to know. Baby, I am dying of cancer. It is too far gone. I couldn't bear you taking this sad journey with me. Don't come to my house. I will not be there. I know, this is tough. I love you, so very much. Baby, just know, you gave me a full life by loving me like you did. I wanted to be with you forever and I was. Goodbye, Love."*

It took some time to heal. She has joined all of my love sources in my image of heaven. I cried my eyes off, then. I cry for my Match, now. I went a while without a woman, after that. Can you blame me? Rest in perfect peace, SAF. I love you.

## A Gangster's Guide To Keeping Her
By Terrance Hutson
### Learning How To Love

Okay. Now. Here we go. We all need help with enlightenment. Whether, it's getting assisted with the information that can enlighten us. Or if the assistance comes well after we've received the enlightening message. When a certain clarity is bestowed upon you. You might have to take some time to process things. I can admit. For me, I need and want a helpmate. I don't want to figure out the rest of life's shit, by myself. I can. But I would prefer not to. I recognized a thing a long time ago. Back when I, first, started wanting to be a better person. I have received a lot of help from others, in a clot of ways, to begin my development. And I'm, so very, thankful for it.

Just by being a witness to the behaviors and stances of those close to me. Or having a real friend calling me out, on my bullshit. Or my original guidance from my life's authorized figures, my parents. I've gained knowledge from each of these avenues. There are folks close to me whose moves I could study. Not jacking their steelo. But I would use what I saw as the 'how?' for me to get going towards my betterment. And I mean a better that requires me to give more to my own self person. To have the ability to love assiduously. It was like I had the love of angels for everything and everybody, but me.

As honest as I've been with you, I can tell you. I don't think I loved me. At all. But why not, though? The answers were right there. Yes. There was more than one answer to my shit. But I didn't see them, immediately. It took a while. Some alone time will help you put a finger on it. By making you deal. I never realized how much and how often, I wasn't tripping off me. I always had somebody else ahead of me, with me. At 17, I basically had a 14 year old son. I was tasked to man up and take care of my younger brother. Legal guardianship and all the shit. I was, already, out on my own. And it was to help lighten my Mom's heavy loads. This was my life. But I was only thinking about my brother then. Plus rent, bills and food were 3 more things atop the 'care for' list. Being that young with the responsibilities of an adult, I couldn't have time for myself. On top of that, I hadn't done shit. So, I didn't know shit. Inevitably, I dropped the ball in some areas of raising my brother and myself. Learning as you're going along, is some bullshit. Let me get an education, prior to or a heads up, at least. Having some knowledge of a situation, is way better than having none. With info, you can make informed, sound decisions. Instead of fucking winging it. Which can open up a whole other path to and of mistakes that I'm not trying to see, again. I had to grow up and learn hella fast. Like plenty other inner city youth. With our single moms working 7000 jobs. She's stupid tired, so her energy is limited to getting ready for job 6,998. Not encouraging you. If she engages you at all. She's telling yo ass what the order of the day is and better be. She's not really able to check on you. Let alone have motivational speeches about loving yourself. On her way to job 6,999.

Out of the teachings I received, I can not recall any of them helping me, love me. Or so I thought. And then, I really started to reflect. I knew to be proud. I knew to protect my siblings. I knew to make particular choices. I knew respect. And I knew that all of this knowing came from a love, for me. To pick up on and use, to be able to love me. Does that make sense? I had to know it to give it. I am being and have been getting taught, thus far. An indirect or subliminal training of soul and psyche. To love myself through loving my family. By helping me pay attention to small and grand examples of, genuine concern. My

Mom was making me familiar with love's magnitudes. I would go on to learn more and more from these, parabolic, lessons taught by my Oracles. Most lessons explained the power in giving a care. Care from the gate. She was sharpening our skills by using our responsibility for one another as a tool. A utensil for understanding what love, looks like. Now, I use the love learned, for me. It enables me to generate an authentic disposition. In my approachability and responsiveness. Okay, now. Ask and answer these few questions, for yourself. What boundaries can be discovered, when we let love lead? Is it limitless? Or does love in action, have a ceiling? Reached by the conditions placed on love? Do you think we can believe in the existence of love, alone? In the attempts to achieve, deliver and receive all of love's purposes. Do you?

    To have a love for self and/or anyone else, you must be clear on your love's purpose. What is that? For you? Your own personal processes, regarding the purpose of you loving. Or even if it's the 'theories to motives' of your partner? Just be clear. For me, the purpose of my love is simple. It's just so you know, I love you. At least, one person loves you, for real. For somebody to be able to trust in that fact, gives me power. It's my love. So, I'm selfish that way. Besides, for others, it provides a, seemingly, unbreakable strength. Adding to the confidence in our relationship. Building the spirit up, to see a full potential, in this life. Loving makes people believe in the 'something' bigger, in all of us. That, once we're awake, thing that pushes us to task 50. At job two. Because our love is responsible for lives. That, good ol', checking on our folks shit. The honesty when asking, "what you need me to do?" Or doing it, without asking. Or, truly, meaning, "call me, if you need anything." That Big Love.

It's purpose is protective. To choose this and do it, proves more than intent. Intent, ain't bad. It just don't mean shit. Most folks won't have ill intentions. Most, intend goodness. But the commitment to love, for real, will demonstrate proof. Providing evidence that this safeguarding is in your communication. From your tone, inflection and word choices. We all get upset. And quick to express it. Which is pretty healthy, to me. But talk to somebody like you care about what happens, after the argument. During the argument. Now, just like that, you're conversing and not barking. Your inflection and word choices, directly affect your delivery. My delivery is trash.

Fucked up, if you will? As told to me by dozens. But not by me, to me. I like me. I like that I do mean my shit, wholeheartedly. I ain't trying to be tough with it, either. I am tough. I can say, mothafuckas is sensitive. But I am too. And more so. Which is a component to my tough. Writing my assessments, right now, is coaching me to 'play' nicer. A work in progress. Again, your delivery can make, break, start or halt a reconciliation. If you no longer enjoy this person, then end it. No one has to suffer from the fact. But if after you've been a hunnud, with yourself. And you want that lover? Practice speaking from your truth.

I know. Being so wide open is spooky and emotionally dangerous. But If I'm going out, I'm going all in. I'd rather lead and lose being for real for real, than a hella hurt ass fake nigga. Fuck that. Risks are in the damn air, these days. I get how reluctant, life and these options can have a person. But your courage to persist is the counterbalance to your diffidence. As the old saying goes, "nothing beats a fail but a try." Not trying to be liked. Not trying to get along. But trying to think better to live better can shift the bad energy you've been receiving. Trying to be in tuned to listen for and staying in position to hear your, specific, directions can keep you safe. At least, in spirit. But what does staying in position and being in tuned, mean? To me, the position is wherever you see yourself doing better. Whether it was in spirit, thinking and in health. Or the trinity. The main goal, is to get to a place where they all exist, in you. Performing in such a locus, with practice and focus, can protect your desires, too. While drawing them nearer and clearer. The 'in tuned' of it, to me, is the everyday attentiveness you communicate to the spirit. It is then translated to your desires. Being in tuned is the use of all of your senses, too. It is the power allowing you to imagine yourself where you want to be. It helps transmit thoughts into reality. Now, transfer this information onto her. Share the ways of refinement with the one you love. What's the worst that can happen? Her coming to the realization of your evolution? She's told you 7000 times what she may need from you. At this point, she's probably ready to tap out, on yo ass.

 These new actions, of yours, hold the promise of reinforcing or reestablishing a good thing. Her, real, love for you will acknowledge your efforts as a testament of your real love for her. It takes regular examples of selflessness to maintain any type of relationship. Almost, all men have a giver's heart. Especially, for his her. He has the readiness to give. But the willingness was a whole different monster, for me. And a giver's heart doesn't, necessarily, mean handing out items or cash. Though, they are well known associates. To keep up the willingness is a hell of a task. It can not be tackled alone. You, as a man, have to see her showing. So, you can keep doing. A man needs to see his her pay attention, listen and use the gems of information he's dropping. We will perform at the highest levels, in love, when we are being motivated by genuinely, convincing acts of reverence. The respect for you must still be there. But what can you do to ensure that she does maintain the respect? Is the answer clear? It was for me. Do the exact same shit you are asking or expecting from her. Duh.

    She is only able to receive your leadership because you trust hers. And she is and has been the lead. We may be the head. But our women have skull drug us in the best directions throughout our history. From war strategies, in the olden days. To navigating through a fucking pandemic, our Oracles are that. Isn't it logical to protect, heal, and cater to the one(s) who do it for you? You must remember the sacrifices she has, always, made, for you all. And let those memories add to the actions of 'Why' you are happy. To say, she is yours is to have a belief in her purpose, in your life. Meaning, your lady was made to help make you. And vice versa. You can not ignore or trivialize the importance of her role, in your life. You chose her to play a part for a reason. I know one, fasho, reason is knowing how right she has kept you. She will specify the detailed steps of the, big picture, you've set out to make real. This is a part of the natural way the unit moves.

# A Gangster's Guide To Keeping Her
By Terrance Hutson
## WTF You Tryna Say

It is, mostly, about clarity. And being understood. I've learned, that 'talking yo shit,' ain't communicating. That it was more of a self-serving attitude. On my bully shit. And not from a respect for any other point of view. My disrespectful ways were unmatched. I'm not proud of that, at all. I, honestly, wasn't shit, then. Especially, when it came to my relationship interests. Again, as I've previously stated. I didn't and couldn't give a fuck. Due to knowing, how you and nobody else can do shit about me, being on my hype. Nobody. Yeah. The arrogance of a piece of shit. Until I sustained some emotional injuries. From 'her'. Probably from the bruises she left across my whole ego. And as an idiot, my first inkling was slap this beezy to sleep. I did not. But my 'snatch yo ass up' game was impeccable. I needed to see her energy up close. To look her in her eyes. To find out where this bullshit was coming from. Plus, I have been tainted by the delusional teachings of what 'man shit' really is. Not offering an excuse for my behavior. Only information to process and use. I thank my God for giving me clearer images of good 'man shit.'

And it was so easy to receive. After, I'd mustered the will to open myself up to a *'possibility'* of me being different. Of being, thinking and feeling better. My God used the beezy and her cold ass language, to slap me. They slapped me schmoove off my high horse. With my cocksure attitude concussed. I awakened to a better way of thinking and being. With a newer outlook and awareness, I felt a healing in my wounded ways. I found myself repaired enough to become a voice of reason. And not of recklessness. I worked on gaining the skill by, constantly, conversing with myself. Which is, basically, a conversation with God in me. Or Prayer. Or talk with my sister and my brother. I knew, with them, it would be easier to begin there. In a neutral zone. Where the judgement was invisible. Where my, real, intentions were known and respected. From there, to my inner circle. Then outer circle. I was able to extend it by, really, talking to the lady in my life. Which was the toughest. I'm sure it was because I stopped being believable, to her. A long time ago. That belief, in me, never returned. And we'd, eventually, split. But not before my attempts to talk to her better exposed me to a comfort in my new methodology. I knew that I'd changed but it was too late.

One thing I have learned. Was, I would talk at mothafuckas. Not, necessarily, to them. I didn't understand what that meant. Or how I was doing it? My logic was, if you're, right the fuck there? In the fuck front of me? Then, punk rock, I'm talking the fuck to you. Fucks wrong witchu? I was, completely, missing the point. The point being, I did more barking than actual communicating. The word communication means to successfully convey ideas and feelings. Or the exchange of information or news. The exchange? So, if my mouth is moving, with words exiting and you don't catch my drift? Or if you are hearing these sounds and that's all they come off as, sounds? Leaving you unable to respond? Or unwilling to respond? We are not communicating. You are, now, being talked at, by me.

It took me to get that, to chill out. To be able to concentrate on more effective ways to relay my intent, point or explanation. But that comprehension was only part of it. Look at this. I feel like I'm about to preach, right here. When needing to make a thing known. How will you know you have? By them hearing you? We all know, hearing ain't listening. How can they, listen? If they can't hear you? Especially, when your words are getting trumped by your, tyrannical delivery? I mean, 'can't hear you,' as in not recognizing, why you might be getting at them. Or the inability to decipher why you're bumping yo yap. Like, damn, what the problem is? Because of your word choices, tone, facial expressions and body language. The crux of it all, is missed or passed over, from the bogus way you got yo shit off. Life and learning is about everybody wanting and needing to get they shit off. Facts. You only, really, get it off the moment another understands. Or a perception has been formed and then announced. Until then. You just fucking with yoself, again.

Our perceptions come about from some sort of stimulation. Once stimulated, we have to compartmentalize or organize the information or news, for processing. The processing leads to our interpretations of what has been received. Now that there is a 'take' developed, it is in our memory. To recall and use what was learned, when faced with this similar or familiar scenario, again. This occurrence happens so often and so quickly, we'd ignore that natural of it. With perception broken down, more respect should be giving to having one and hearing one. Simply because, with you, the view was shared. It doesn't mean you have to agree with said view.

Nor should you respond, as if, others can't have or believe in their own way. It's kind of on some, just be glad in having the exchange. And you guys are getting somewhere with the discussion.

But what if your interpretation of what is being said, don't match? Now what? What are possible causes of that? Well, for one. You may have made her disconnect. With your delivery. And now, she's not able to listen. It goes back to word choices and all the shit. By now, you should pick up on the importance of good communication practices. If she still hasn't grasped your point and she hasn't come off to you, like fuck yo point? There is still time and room to transmit your message. All of this shit works both ways. As long as she is a part of the loving. She has her fucking part, too.

Then you may have the possibility of lines being crossed, clogged or clipped. Crossed lines is a term I use when you, both, are saying the same thing but the barking is too loud to notice the foul. Just remain mindful that crossed lines will occur with like minded people. It is going to sound different, on the sole fact of opposites. Being man and woman. The act of clipped lines is pretty self explanatory. You cut off! Ain't nobody listening to shit 'cause attitudes got y'all not saying shit. If it was a chance to reconcile? You all have fucked that up, by being stubborn. Or lame as hell. Either way, both of y'all acting like some bitches.

Now, clogged lines deserves its own book. But I'm gonna just finger it for you. Not go all in. The clog has more underlying issues to it. And both of you need to take a look at a few things. Because, for some reason, shit's not getting through. To either of you. Don't get scared. The clog is not the sign you've been praying to see, "if this ain't what God wants for me," face ass. I do think it's God reminding you that there is still work to do. A pure, good love lives forever, unconditionally. With that fact, a lover's job should never be over. So, tighten the fuck up. Jog y'all memories. Relight the flame. This is not where you part ways. This is where you start to look at what causes clogging?

One, the angle or approach isn't, clearly, understood by one of you. Your delivery is calm. Your words are being selected with a care. But the topic itself is a doozy to deal with. Death, breaking up, lying or cheating fall under difficult subject matter categories. From the feeling of confrontation to taking blows from the disappointment of others. Most of us would want to tiptoe around the issues. Why? Because we have not been trained or shown, any, examples of decent communication. There was the yeller, the yelled at and the yelled around. The dictator and the sufferers. And a lot of us still need to be healed from that kind of past. So our talking abilities still suck. This guide is to help you discover our similar traumas. Or whether they are very dissimilar, it is to help recognize the foul shit in our upbringing and bring something better up out of that. By deciding to do some things opposite of what you've seen, gives you a better chance at surviving. And more than making it, through life, love and an argument.

    Two, the thoughts or feeling of disrespect being aimed at you or your way of believing. I have been left alone because of my logic behind what I believe. Although, I offered my will to find a median. Or the words to use to get her to see the sense in my way, for me. But that was the problem. My shit working for me, is simply that. It works, for me. She shouldn't knock it. And don't impose the full weight of my ways on a her. The attempt is offensive as the fuck, by itself. Talking to each other will help you. Or the circumstances surrounding the situation. These are all direct influences on the clog.

Have you ever shared info with somebody? You start the conversation off from an, intentionally, good place. Then, all of the sudden, you are in full fuss mode? If so? One of the three previous reasons caused the shift. And, in my mind, there is one preventative measure to stop any clogging. All you really have to do is, hold an awareness of the commitment to make sense. Both of you. When the focus is making things, click together, the team wins. You two will have disagreements and different view points. It's okay. Being a man. You are, definitely, on the other side. Not an enemy. Simply, the counterpart. But you are supposed to be. Because the more contributions, each of you, give to the business of loving. The less confusion. The clearer expectations and guidelines. The righter the decisions. For the unit. The team. Leading to a purer understanding in your talks about finances, the relationship, raising children and spirituality. It's how this life thing is balanced.

# A Gangster's Guide To Keeping Her
By Terrance Hutson
## Know You, You Know

Here's something I've, always, told my son. Knowing what he's about, what he needs and his purpose, makes life easier. Whether he spent most of his time pondering what that looks like. Or he, instantly, recognized the examples before him. He's protected by the power in knowing himself. Knowing he is the deciding factor in his life. Because he knows how much he matters. And it comes with the ability to count up his worth. That helps to see the value in others or their deficit. So, tune in to you. Because, you, are the only thing you may ever, truly, know. For real. I mean, granted everything is situational. But off top. Should you even be in some shit that you are not you in? Fuck No. That goes for friendships, earning and dating. I, also, tell him to focus on his now for a future. The more his shit is together. The more space or room, in his heart and mind to find one hundred ways, to show her. Shout out James Ingram. I'd promote getting himself squared away. Spiritually and financially. Because with those two down, he's well on the way to being and staying straight. This can apply to anybody that's wondering how to have a real life.

I will be there for him. So he doesn't fall. Or if he does.

I shall say unto you, the same. Before there is even a consideration for a lover. There needs to be a concern for you. By you. One of the realest phrases, ever is 'how/why would somebody love you, if you don't love yourself.' However, the folks that said that, never shared the procedures of how to love ourselves, with us. The first thing I needed to find out, was where to start. Like you, I feel like I taught myself how to think of me. How to be okay with me. And to trust me. How? By being honest with myself. About my future. My thinking, how and who I am. I speak to me, from the inside. I had to acknowledge my weaknesses and my, real, power. Knowing your strengths will help, eventually, cure or solve your issues with your inadequacies. Some of what we may consider flaws, can be the same things that make you one of a kind. Don't worry too much with that. Instead, direct your thoughts to the traits and ways you find likeable, about you.

Only, after, you've spent time on your personal development and growth, may you start your search for your 'her'. Picture her. Who is she? As a person? What does she believe? How will she add to you? And you, to her? How does she have to be? As far as temperament and character. There are a gang of intentional ass questions you have to ask, when you are claiming to be ready for this life. You, as the man, can't cut these corners. You should, not only, be as open as you need her to be. But also, the example of whatever energy she needs to have. Meaning, let her see why/how she is able to answer and ask anything, too. You have to create an emotionally safe environment, for her. The understanding for patience and the patience to understand, have to be a good part of who you know you are. And just be genuine. If it's cool. Let it be cool. If not? Can you mend it? Do you need to talk it out? There's no need to blow things out of proportion when expressing discomfort. Be truthful. Give her information that leaves her with a choice. At all times.

And don't sweat the small shit. It only magnifies the flaws you tried to mask, with your outbursts. We are all imperfect humans. We make mistakes. But mistakes are different from flat out fucking up. I mean, let's be real. Confusion causes both. But communicating to get it, to understand what's being mentioned, has a healthy chance of killing both. A mistake can be forgiven. And continue on, in a good thing. A fuck up, though? I'm not strong enough for that. I don't want to be, either. Some mistakes are from the past. Everybody has a past. Don't let what used to be interfere with what is.

Relationships come with stirs of emotions and sensitive topics that invoke more. More emotions like. Jealousy, trustworthiness, doubt, self esteem and fear, just to name a few. From the grading of appreciation to the weight of your believability. There are factors that depend on your consistency. The only ways to display the necessary consistency. Is one, you are pure with your intent to have this love. Or two, you can act yo ass off. And everybody's tired of you playful niggas, acting. I can't get nobody cool, 'cause y'all playing and shit, hella much, make ladies group us all together. To them, we all are. Then she starts to grade your appreciation of/for her. The lower the mark, the less she believes you. Prevent the possibility of a mishap, like this, by being hella sure before entering her life. Or before inviting her into yours. Be sure you've prepared your trinity (spirit, heart and mind) to receive hers. And be accepted. Starting with true confidence, in you, first. Then her. And finally, the union. This will take the shit out of the game. Surely so, when you are an active participant in your choices. Remember. Be confident. Not arrogant. To her, real confidence is some sexy shit.

# A Gangster's Guide To Keeping Her
By Terrance Hutson
**You chose her**

Things are easier than we choose to believe. I used the word choose because we, sometimes, find the nerves to act like we forgot that we chose this shit. You was wide awake when you put them, uglass, shoes on this fucking morning. To match that, uglass, shirt. Wasn't you? Witcho, Uglass. It wasn't a power outage. You saw that shit and chose. Choosing is one action that has several, telling outcomes. Choosing allows others to see your level of surety. It can, expose the flaws in your thinking. Or give indication to your mood. You wouldn't pick a shoe size you couldn't fit. But you would select between reading or watching television. Depending on what you wanted to do. Do you know what you want?

Coming across a person that does it for you, is dreamy as the heavens. With all sorts of 'feelings' involved. How do you determine if she,"does it for you," or are you feeling something else, entirely? How can you tell? Acknowledge the inquiry, with, "I don't know or I've never thought of it." Or something of a reply. Not a, lowly, response. I hate when I ask a question and folks answer with a question. Anyway. The eyes send the messages and the heart reads the notes. This part of your system is bluetoothing, right now. Signals translate what's seen into thoughts and feelings. Then Actions. There is a power, being chemically released to connect the two energies. Basically, the opposite forces fused, together, both of your internal compatibilities. Giving you the blessings or the okay, to work on making the rest work.

Brother. Don't let yourself deal with the thinking and your feelings on your own. Once you can say to yourself, " I like her." Go tell her. How she responds only gives up a slight clue to the mutuality. If, she is interested. If she is, listen to her word choices. Pay attention to how your system reacts to her words. Let your system hear your reactions before they even reach your tongue to leave yo face. A lot can be gained and avoided, just by using some awareness. Some self respect and tact, also, go a long way. These things can keep you calm enough to focus on the mattering. Which is, keeping her. Keeping her cool. Keeping her coming to you. Keeping her yours. Being overwhelmed by her physical appearance is not love. It's yo nerd ass acting like a beauty don't need a beast. Being attracted to her does not constitute grounds for a coupling. It helps. But nah, fam. Don't fuck with yourself like that. You chose her and she chose you back. Liking her this much, deserves honesty and respect. Loving her is protection and patience. Caring for her produces an infatuation and romance. The trustworthiness in your wording, when conversing with her, she admires you for it. She understands the ways that you talk to her is tied to the respect you have for her. She believes, if you have and are willing to make conscious efforts to think before you speak. She will help you feel safe to keep it going. As her man, you're ready to, physically, protect her. But that's not the only kind of security she needs. Financially? Yes. But protect her by keeping her sure. She should be sure, you still want this. For as long as this is still the truth for you. Sure that you will come to her, first. Sure that you are sure about her and her intentions. The care is exposed through the kindnesses expressed for her. It's part of the reason why he can't walk by you or passed you without touching you somewhere, somehow. All of these manners of behavior are prime examples of making love, the whole day. You chose. Love yourself for your choice.

    Trust me, when I say, ain't shit out here in these streets, big fella. I been out in them. And as a hella single man, I do want a lady friend in my life. But things and times are so different. If it isn't a fuck ass conversation about fake shit. It'll be how much she doesn't need a man. Or how much bread she needs. The shit has shifted out here. Seeming to have gotten me confused with these weird ass, lil pants, tricking ass, dope fiend ass new niggas. Hoe. I'm an Island. You bitch, you. Between you money grubbing, bops hooking under the guise of "models," and these monkey ass mitches and murses. This is no country for old niggaz. I'm cool. It's just a fool out here, nowadays. Again, today's woman has found less need for a man like me. They're not interested in the caring of a lover. No. Because they are making more time for bullshit. Hold on to your one, fam. You chose her.

# A Gangster's Guide To Keeping Her
By Terrance Hutson
## I Tried. Hella Times

Just recently, I was talking with an old flame. One of many, I tried to see if a spark was still available. I was, pleasingly, shocked by the call. Oh shit! She'd called me, of all folks, after hella years. I didn't reach out to her. She called. Maybe that meant, it's sparky. And I only say, "of all folks," because of the time lapse. Now, she was my one, back in the days. Presently, she is 'my was'. Anyway, she didn't sound like her regular self. You know how you can hear shit in that person's voice? She seemed upset about something. I pried a bit. She opened up. And told me she needed a real friend to vent to. I obliged because first, it's her. Second, talking people down is another one of my callings. 'My was' started spilling her guts, teary eyed and grief-struck, she barely took a breath. The gist of the matter, is she caught her boyfriend of several years, cheating. Live and in color. It was crushing her. I was pissed. Not at her. But her pain. Not what caused it. But its existence.

I never hated on the fucking fool. I just listened to her. When I could, I took the opportunities to make her laugh. On that call, I began to reminisce. Talking the olden days can do that. I mean, I was single. So we entertained the thoughts for a minute or three. It helped her think about something other than hurting. It made me feel like I wasn't, alone alone. We were on the phone for a few hours. I big enjoyed it. For my own self person. I kept checking on her through the following weeks, trying to lift her up. And then, abruptly, she stopped. No answer. No responses. Just a vanishing. She popped up a few weeks later. She was different. Good? Bad? I'm not sure, which. She was, really, destroyed by the cheater. So, maybe she had to shut down to power up. Only she knows. In our talk, after her hiatus, she tried to explain her choices. I didn't want to hear it. Not trying to be an asshole. It just didn't matter. But I must have come off like one. An asshole. And she proceeded to tell me, why she could never fuck with me. After, my attempts to bring her back from hurt's hell. This is my reward? Wow.

    She had basis for her rejection. She was protecting herself and her energy. Not from me. But just for her. Which is one of the ten rules to this game, of real ass life. Protect yourself at all times. But I didn't want to hear that shit. My, 'fuck allat' ways needed more efforts to be understood. Because I never judged her. Didn't tell her, 'fuck what you talkin' bout!' Never called her a dumb ass for being cheated on. I didn't tell her, what I couldn't do or can't fool with. No rulings, at all. I wouldn't. I am not made like that. Yet, my ability to be, neutrally, on your side will never see reciprocation. I speak on these things, to give you an idea of how it has gone for me. I get a particular treatment because I have always been 'looked' at a particular way. I am not you niggas. I am of another realm. Folks don't know how to take me. I am never taken as I am. So, on earth, I may never have a life with a wife. Unless, a her, from my species comes to rescue me. But back to my point. I see, feel, listen, think of and about things differently. Your way or ways aren't bad. I know you are a, fairly, decent person, you are reading this book. I take that as you are aware of your desires to want to keep her. For your real reasons. With you and I combining forces, at least, You can win by using what you can, from this guide.

    I have tried, hella times, to be with somebody. I am probably going to keep trying. Because that is how I am Made. And I know me. And for me, the more and more I grow, the better I will fit her, when she shows up. And the better my odds. At the present moment, I am preparing myself for my her to arrive, again. Now, when she does, I have my understandings on how to keep her. But how will I know she still wants to be kept? I won't. And that is the good bad part. I mean, there are actors and pretenders everywhere, man. I have been duped before. But prior to finding out, everything was all good. She made me believe. The acting will not sustain. People can not remain the same, when living in love's lies. Their true colors will show, eventually. That eventually shit and the not knowing for sure, those are the bad of it. Thankfully, It didn't take hella invested time for me to see the real. Not all of us are this fortunate. As strong as I am in my discernment. Her performance was award winning. I fell, fast. Fonky dog head wanch. As I watched the show. I'm not sure if she was seeing somebody else, or not. I did start to notice the differences in her interactions with me. The mentally and emotionally settling talks, she'd initiate, were disappearing. The amount of time spent. Live and in person or on the phone, was cut short. She had more of an attitude. Regular shit would get inflated into bullshit, gas bubbles. And she'd explode. I tried to ask the right questions, for understanding. But when she is there. I couldn't even, accidentally, stumble upon the right shit to ask. Because bullshitting doesn't have an answer for it. I tried to compromise. I tried to allow some space. I, also, attempted to get words of advice from her parents and sister. Nope. Everybody knew the sham, the game, the fix was in, but me. It is a cold ass game. More so, for a team player. And I still want a life with one, I can claim as my her.

# A Gangster's Guide To Keeping Her
By Terrance Hutson
## You are the center of it all

As the center of it all, you, can't play. Plus, you, can't have yo ass in the way. Meaning, both of those 'can nots', are not, you. The center is the supplier. The feeder. And the Gift. The duties hit different when accepting these executive roles. Yes. These important and powerful roles. Because both of you guys are responsible for managing, directing, and coordinating the emotional equity of the partnership. However, I am speaking more to the comprehensive abilities of bruh. You control the overall operations and functionalities of the union. What helps you become a leader of loving, is making the collective's goal, result in happiness. Happiness is one form of residuals of you relating. There are several systems of service for your internal revenue. For example, we have effective communication, understanding, protection, affection and a team oriented way.

As a manager, you are able to place certain behaviors, where needed. If there was a disagreement, between you two. You would call on compromise to aid in bringing you all back, to goodness. In a misunderstanding, you would contract care to revive clarity. You are not running around barking orders just because you have a position in management. No. You know and respect the power you have. Because she gave it to you. Just as you bestowed power unto her. And it is as simple as knowing, you both, could've said no. But the word, Yes is a power source and charger. When you use it. Manage to keep hearing her. And listening to her. It's her heart you hear. She's telling you, exactly, what she needs. The beauty in being so tapped in with, your, her, is that you can believe in her truth. She's not playing you with you. There is a purpose tied into the things she's trying to tell you. She knows you're not playing with her. So, as soon as you get where she's coming from, manage to acknowledge that you do. Don't rebuttal it, with trying to make your point. Please don't. Not that you can't have a point or express it. No. Remember, you are still being conscious of hearing her. Your acknowledgement is acting on what was heard. And that action is you listening.

    The center is a supplier. You should be providing sense/logic, protection, passion and your whole or half part. I'm going to go a little out of order but you'll be all right. Your whole or half, is referring to the business part of the relationship. The agreement. This, right here, is for the couples who live together. Are you bringing anything to the table? It is, quite, off putting to love someone. But can't bask in the happy feelings, because of a severe case of the 'brokes'. The illness can be cured. But it can be fucked up between y'all until it is. Again, have yo part before you guys become the one. What is your financial responsibility? If you've agreed to pay all the household expenses? Then put the work in and keep your end of the deal. This is directly related to the trust, security and the degree of pride she's giving to you. Believe me. A loving pairing is full of fucking deals. For the compromise. And it should be. That is part of the sense it makes to be in love with her. The, "in love, with her," makes it dumb ass easier to feel the deals that should be made. Even if she has tripped out on you and it seems she is missing the logic. She might be missing it, for real. But she holds a high regard for you. For always wanting the things, you feel or those of your ways, to make sense to her. Which, in turn, keeps her willing to keep making those, important deals with you, too. And you supply that. Time and again. She should tell you more often. But she does appreciate you for it.

You should keep her fed full of that DICK! You are the feeder. Feed Her That DICK! Nah. I'm kind of kidding. But not. Any who. Keep her full of that time. Timing is or could be, everything. Feed her some of your attention. Engage her. A genuine interest in some of the details of your lady's life or ways, should be natural. But as men, we are so King Shit based, how we are treated can have us lose focus. And we are so dumb, at times, we seem to forget, King Shit comes with and from, Queen Shit. I, almost, left 'the spend time talk' out. Because duh. Motherfucker. None of this shit gone mean shit, if you ain't around the mothafucka. But. Yeah. Give her the royal treatment. The same as you believe you deserve. She has earned it. Pay attention to all of the ways how you know she has earned it.

And feed her useful information, too. Having her laced or gamed up in a similar fashion, only solidifies the unit. Her background or walk may be different. It does not matter. Because an understanding of each others belief systems out of respect is a, real, foundation. The saying, 'let's build,' has duality. Enhancing each other and improving the future. If you need to? Adopt this ideology to ensure its importance lives in your actions. The strength of the structure, as a whole, relies, greatly, on the foundation. What is built right there, on solid ground, will withstand. And grow.

## A Gangster's Guide To Keeping Her
By Terrance Hutson
### That Shit Could've Been Avoided

Have you ever considered how important spending time is, to your person? Or just think of how important time is, period. Oh, to have enough time. Time loss. Time zones. Nah. I'm fucking around. But time is, closely, tied to the belief in the level of your care, for her. Too busy, is not a thing. Being busy is, though. But if you are that busy? Why would you subject a person to this selfishness? You just want them to sit there, waiting for you to decide to make the time? That's fucked up. I know every situation ain't the same. Some jobs, careers and entrepreneurial endeavors are quite demanding. Here is when you have to be honest, as shit, with yourself. Then her. Regarding the combination. If not. One or both parties will be stressed the fuck out. And pissed. Mainly because the whole shit could have been avoided. Now, I can see if your scenario switched. And your job, the hours or location changed in the middle of loving on somebody. I can see you asking her to hang in there, as you guys adjust. I can, also, see her needing you to send an extra call or text. So, she can have reason to believe in us. And, if she's able to witness the team effort? She can calm herself in, another, part of security that you are providing.

We make time for the things we want. And need. If your dream is bigger than the relationship? Then, let the truth be known. You'd never know. She may be willing or able to play a different role, for the success of the team. Or she may even wait for you. Just leave her with an option. Don't take it away, by making decisions without including her. You guys, may not ever heal from the indignation. Which flows into resentment. And resentment to disdain. Now, a different set of eyes are set on you. And they see you as wrong. From the, perceived, lack of respect regarding your unfair practices. Respect, is the road to avoid the unnecessary. It, also, adds to a trusting that this is a good place. And you, really, want to go there.

You have found a great thing. You've done what many folks said you wouldn't or couldn't do. Maybe, you've even said it about yourself. And that is ending your selfish ass cycle. Who'd ever think that the type of fellow you are, could be seen in such a light? Your egotistical history of unchanging, kept you in the shadows. Hidden from your own self person. Until you step into your shininess, the repetition of asking why this again? Will continue haunting you with a familiar pain. I've convinced myself, that a self-serving approach is a self preserving action. But the truth was opposite. I've caused me more hurt than any other person ever has. I protected me but not us. And that is grounds for a definite fail.

The appreciated will, always, appreciate. I'm gonna let that thang breathe for a minute. Yeah. Yeah. The appreciated, will appreciate. Ugh! That's deep. Are you being appreciated? Do you know what it feels like? Are you appreciative? I wanna know. Well, appreciation includes several factoring aspects, to its realness. The recognition of value. The increase. From the praise to the gratitude. It's like a gumbo of goodness, mixed together for your person. Seeing their value is why you want to add to it. The increase makes you apart of something bigger. And now yo sucka ass selfish shit is leaving and getting out of y'all way. Making more space to give and get praises. As one of the ways to expressing your gratitude. All the good things of your desires shall be gained. Just do good.

I used to think being slick, lying and having angles was the simplest way to live. I could count, on one hand, how many times I'd tell yo ass a truth. Not my truth. A truth. I used to think I was obligated to, only, me. I guess, I've developed the ways of a pure asshole. If you believe/believed I am controlling the scenarios, you can't do shit about me, me-ing. Only a fool would try. Yet, I was still experiencing the same outcomes. With different costars but the exact same script. And still kept wanting better endings, each shows' time. That shit dumb as the fuck. Bruh. I hate being dumb. So, the first way I began the difference was I stopped lying. And started to be more informative. From there, I just wanted to be and do better. We made a song a few years ago (available on all platforms) titled, D.R.U.G.S. Do Right U Get Success. By Ivy League M.A.F.I.A. This was recorded well after I'd decided to live as an example. Not only did the meaning of/for the song change my life. The ways of the song are mine. And I use that, to this day, to alter the lives around me.

Again, we all have the power to positively or negatively impact a life. But one way just, automatically, makes more sense than the other. Anything other than the obvious, you are in the fucking way. I hate thinking I'm in the way. Or feeling like I'm bothering you. I don't want to be annoying. Bugging the shit out of you, to me, is the most felonious offense, one can commit.

Especially, when they've been annoyed with yo mothafuckin' ass. But you just finding out. That gotta suck worm penis. And nobody wants that. The contempt, for you, being displayed from an underlying pique, may start to resemble hatred. Now, the love you've labored in, has hired abhorrence as the replacement. I can't say that I have or have I known anyone that mended their relationship, after being removed so far away from their love. I've seen valiant attempts towards it. The promises to never do it again. The feeling like the slightest thing could put us back in jeopardy. Fake-givings. Saying they forgave you but not forgetting. Without success. Because the damage and all that shit could have been avoided.

# A Gangster's Guide To Keeping Her
By Terrance Hutson
### The Gift
*Love's tongue speaks to love's life*
*In love's ear in love's time*
*I love my love is mine*
*Because I keep love on love's mind*

The expressions of affection, go way beyond any physical elements. The Libra in me, knows this to be fact. I am, innately, charming as fuck. But by the number of women that think I'm full of shit. I know you mothafuckas ain't talking, yo, shit. Or like I said, you niggas is lying hella much. Not too long ago, this young lady said she didn't trust me. Because, 'you, always say the right shit. You too smooth with it too. It's like there's no effort in it, at all.' This fucked me up. I'm like, I don't get it. I mean, not on no Latimore shit, as if I can't understand, anything. But more like, what could possibly be wrong with hearing the right shit, all the time? From a mothafucka, saying the right shit, all the time. I do not get that. And if I pulled back, she would turn it around. Asking me, 'what happened to all that sweet shit you used to say to me?' Ain't that about a bitch.

Anyways, my ability to express my thinking. My emotional space and time. And how, fluently,

I can speak my and other love languages, makes me capable of being, not you niggas. I am, naturally, this. It is the thing that most men need some sort of practice in performing. But it is there, Fam. In you. We just don't pay attention to it, as easily. Because the goodness is, simply, happening. We use terms of endearment, everyday B. With our children, parents, potnas, other rellos and cuzzos. Even fucking strangers. Yet, the first person that should get it, she, gets never minded. Is this done, Intentionally? I don't believe so. I think the employment(making use of) rate for men, regarding affection, is neck and neck with the job market for Black men. So, as men. We must make her our business. You know how hard it is to get the job, like the job and keep the job. Shiiiid. Go invest energies into yo business, of her.

Part of investing, is keeping her in the loop of these executive decisions, of loving. Can you be honest about your fears, with her? She may be as spooked as you. You both might find that that commonality, eased away your fears. Do you, only, let her know the good, you see? Are you, even, comfortable in that capacity? If not does she know, you're not? Does she deal with it from an understanding take? Or does she execute a controller's tactic? Is she a, 'you should be like this, mouth ass chick or a you can't be like that,' smelling ass female? These are real questions. The answers are indicators of her good ministration or mistreatment, of you. Think of them as the telling signs or red flags of your protection. Ignore them and yo ass is gonna be hurting, like a mug. When the gift of hindsight reminds you that you saw, heard and felt the urge. The urge to check the situation before it got out of hand. Or the urge to correct it and you did nothing.

    It is essential for each of you, to work on your handlebars. How do you guys handle the newly found knowledge, that can drop out of the sky, on y'all monkey ass? Does the frustration(s) quickly result into a fight fight? Or is the approach to exasperation, a delicate one? On egg shells? Or one of an automatic resolve? Your handling of the issue or the problem, will make or break the bond. Any and every choice can be detrimental to a couple's survival. Try to always keep that and this in mind. The more good shit you are able to stay conscious of, the better chance you guys have, towards your desired outcomes. It adds a little direction on how to handle things. No one's perfect. The only right answer is what the pair has faith in choosing. What's best for the unit's, overall, well being? Is the group's only consideration or concern. By tapping into a lover's resources like your thoughtfulness, the team mentality and a trusting spirit. And keep the awareness when handling the tough topics of love's looks at life's lessons. You will be able to let love lead.

Of course, there are other factors and angles to keeping her. There could be more talks on selfishness, patience, emotional fitness and gentleness. I could have offered hella more pages on liking her, alone. But in the grand scheme of things, this guide's duty is just that. To guide. To set you off on your path, to keeping her. The repetitious mentioning and various ways to say, 'just keep talking to her. Has been drilled in because the answers to resolve or a good ending, is in your communication. Another part of the ability is giving what you need. Not necessarily what you expect. While listening to what she has shared with you, as far as her needs. Be kinder. Be more mindful of the other's side. Be honest about your fears, changes, understanding and desires. Know that your energy can and will be matched. For better and for worse. Give your lady great examples to imitate or mimic or adapt.

This love thing is a treat of life. It lends a strength in life's hardest times. It has the power to repair, a many, torn relationships. And make them whole, again. You become a 'keeper' the moment you love in the truth.

    Yes. Loving and being loved are, both, gifts. The ability to love is a true blessing. One of the best times in a life, is when you've found your person. I'm cheesing just thinking about, when. There is a pure joy in seeing and feeling like, somebody has noticed you. And them wanting what you have to offer. Now, think about some of the things having a love allows you to see and do. The reason and way you light up when you are around or get to talk to your person. The beauty in the anxiety. The adorableness hiding inside the shyness. The nostalgia of newness, reminding you of the innocence in liking. I remember having a good nervousness on our dates. Back when I had somebody. I couldn't go anywhere, without thinking of her. So bad, when I would go to the mall, I'd grab her something first or too. I used to love picking up our favorite little foods on my way in. Even just calling to say I'm on my way, baby. Or the 'otw' text. That was the shit to me. Being her go to and having one, for your own self person, was a prize in itself. I miss being trusted. Loved. Thought of. I miss turning her on by making love to her, all day. Through our daily interactions, out of our adoration for one another. I miss being apart of reciprocation's realizations. Watching the favors of loving return. Then reoccur. "There's nothing better than love." Word to Luther and Gregory. Seeing your way to love reflects a likeness, in the spirit of your person. What's better than that? Just to get a peek of those expressions, makes you want to replay love's scenes, over and over.

All of love's allowances are gifts worth cherishing. Between the physical perks and emotional celebrations of loving, life can feel special. Respect these graces given unto you. Respect them, first, by showing you know that this thing did not have to be yours. By knowing the time shared, could've, easily, not chimed in. Respect being a receiver. In turn, you may find yourself, naturally, being a respected giver. And rock like you know that your presence is a present. Shout out Darlene Ortiz(5150), for that one. But it is as easy as that. Fucking, just be there. Fall through. Or like the kids say these days, pull up. When where you are, is where you want to be, is the same place you should be. Everybody's a winner, bruh. She can sense you wanting to be around her. The sensation, may refill her heart's cup, back, full of a joy, that you remember. By you seeing her joy, you should inherit your own sort of replenishing. The willingness, the ability, the desire, the feeling, the action, the right and the power in loving, truly, are all of God. Residing in you, to be exemplified by you. Making you, your person and anybody who loves, The Gift.

**I Thank You.**
**I See You.**
**I Love You.**

The Following Are Lyrics From A Song I Wrote.

## "Everything Is Okay, Now"

I didn't want to be left again, stressing in deafening cries

Yelling out, why oh why, I keep failing at tries

And just at the moment my lonely focus, only wanted me to stay blind

The light of my life, she shined on me and she was right on time(right on time)

Putting us here, baby, we right here, where a goodness appeared

And over what was lost for this find, I shouldn't've feared(because I shouldn't have fear)

What is so clear, Everything is okay, now

The truth has fought its way out and it caught me on my way down

**Chorus:** And it's okay. It's okay. For you and me

You say you wanted some peace, I got yo ease and I believe

I believe it's okay for you and me, you been blessed with all yo wants and needs

What I don't meet, I'm gon be and you gone see

Everything is okay, now

In Perfect,
Loving Memory
Of
My Aunt
# Edna Faye Thomas
You are loved, cherished and missed.

Thank You Forever, Auntie!

www.ingramcontent.com/pod-product-compliance
Lightning Source LLC
Chambersburg PA
CBHW071744040426
42446CB00012B/2473